This
Treasure Cove Story
belongs to
TCS
TCS

FINDING DORY

A CENTUM BOOK 978-1-912396-92-4
Published in Great Britain by Centum Books Ltd.
This edition published 2021.

1 3 5 7 9 10 8 6 4 2

Centum Books Ltd, 20 Devon Square, Newton Abbot, Devon, TQ12 2HR, UK.
9/10 Fenian St, Dublin 2, D02 RX24, Ireland.

www.centumbooksltd.co.uk | books@centumbooksltd.co.uk
CENTUM BOOKS Limited Reg. No. 07641486.

A CIP catalogue record for this book is available from the British Library.

Printed in China.

A Treasure Cove Story

Adapted by
Amy Novesky

Illustrated by
Satoshi Hashimoto

Designed by
Tony Fejeran

This is Dory.

Dory is **forgetful.**

When Dory was young, her parents collected **shells** and made trails for her to follow so she would always find her way home.

One day, Dory spotted a pretty **purple shell** in the distance. She wasn't allowed to swim that far. But Dory forgot.

Dory was just about to pick up the shell when –

WHOOSH!

– she was pulled away by the current.

Suddenly, Dory was **all alone**.

She **couldn't** find her way home.

Eventually, she forgot what she was looking for. No one was able to help.

And then she crashed into **Marlin**. Marlin was far from home, too. He was looking for his son, Nemo.

Dory helped Marlin cross the ocean and find Nemo. She went to live with them in the coral reef. She finally had a new **home**.

One day, Dory went with Nemo's class on a field trip to see the **stingray migration**. Dory got pulled into the current!

When Dory returned to safety, she was flooded with **memories** of her mum and dad.

She **remembered** where she was from! Dory wanted to go home.

With the help of some **old friends**, Marlin and Nemo joined Dory on her trip **across the ocean**...

...all the way to Morro Bay, where she was **scooped up** and

taken
away!

Dory found herself in a tank
inside the **Marine Life Institute**.
This was where she was from.

A **cranky** septopus,
a seven-armed octopus, named
Hank greeted Dory and agreed
to help her find her family.
He had three hearts, after all.

But Dory was tossed into the Whale Shark pool, which is where Dory met **Destiny**.

When Destiny heard Dory speak Whale, she couldn't believe it.

When Dory lived at the Marine Life Institute, Dory and Destiny had been **pipe pals**! They used to talk through the pipes that connected their tanks.

Destiny knew where Dory had grown up!

'Your Whale has got really good,' Destiny said.

Hank soon joined them. Dory told Destiny and her neighbour, **Bailey**, a beluga whale, that she was looking for her family.

Destiny told Dory to take the pipes to the **Open Ocean exhibit**. That was where she would find her family.

Dory was worried she would get lost in the pipes, so she found another way.

Hank and Dory

rolled …

… **swam** …

...and **swung** across the Institute to the Open Ocean exhibit.

Dory was sad to say **goodbye** to Hank. She would miss him. But he wanted to go to Cleveland.

'You'll forget me in a heartbeat. Three heartbeats. Now go and find your family,' said Hank.

Dory asked around for help, but no one knew where her family was. Then she saw something.

Dory found her house! But it was **empty**.

Suddenly, Dory was filled with memories. She remembered her mum and dad hugging her. She had to find them!

Dory spotted a **purple shell** in the distance.

As she swam towards it, she met a **crab** who told her if she went through the pipes, she would find her parents.

She followed the directions and ended up in the ocean!

She was all alone again.

Dory worried that she'd never find her way home. Then she spotted another shell and another.

Dory followed
a trail of **Shells** ...

... and she found her
mum and **dad**!

Dory was home again, surrounded by her **family** and all of her friends.

Treasure Cove Stories

Please contact Centum Books to receive the full list of titles in the *Treasure Cove Stories* series. books@centumbooksltd.co.uk

1 Three Little Pigs
2 Snow White and the Seven Dwarfs
3 The Fox and the Hound - Hide-and-Seek
4 Dumbo
5 Cinderella
6 Cinderella's Friends
7 Alice in Wonderland
8 Mad Hatter's Tea Party from Alice in Wonderland
9 Mickey Mouse and his Spaceship
10 Peter Pan
11 Pinocchio
12 Mickey and the Beanstalk
13 Sleeping Beauty and the Good Fairies
14 The Lucky Puppy
15 Chicken Little
16 The Incredibles
17 Coco
18 Winnie the Pooh and Tigger
19 The Sword in the Stone
20 Mary Poppins
21 The Jungle Book
22 Aristocats
23 Lady and the Tramp
24 Bambi
25 Bambi - Friends of the Forest
26 Pete's Dragon
27 Beauty and the Beast - The Teapot's Tale
28 Monsters, Inc. – M is for Monster
29 Finding Nemo
30 The Incredibles 2
31 The Incredibles – Jack-Jack Attack
33 Wall-E
34 Up
35 The Princess and the Frog
36 Toy Story – The Pet Problem
39 Spider-Man – Night of the Vulture!
40 Wreck it Ralph
41 Ralph Breaks the Internet
42 The Invincible Iron Man – Eye of the Dragon
45 Toy Story – A Roaring Adventure
46 Cars – Deputy Mater Saves the Day!
47 Spider-Man – Trapped by the Green Goblin
49 Spider-Man – High Voltage!
50 Frozen
51 Cinderella is my Babysitter
52 Beauty and the Beast - I am the Beast
56 I am a Princess
57 The Big Book of Paw Patrol
58 Paw Patrol - Adventures with Grandpa!
59 Paw Patrol - Pirate Pups!
60 Trolls
61 Trolls Holiday
63 Zootropolis
64 Ariel is my Babysitter
65 Tiana is my Babysitter
66 Belle is my Babysitter
67 Paw Patrol - Itty-Bitty Kitty Rescue
68 Moana
70 Guardians of the Galaxy
71 Captain America - High-Stakes Heist!
72 Ant-Man
73 The Mighty Avengers
74 The Mighty Avengers - Lights Out!
75 The Incredible Hulk
78 Paw Patrol - All-Star Pups!
80 I am Ariel
82 Jasmine is my Babysitter
87 Beauty and the Beast - I am Belle
88 The Lion Guard - The Imaginary Okapi
89 Thor - Thunder Strike!
90 Guardians of the Galaxy - Rocket to the Rescue!
93 Olaf's Frozen Adventure
95 Trolls - Branch's Bunker Birthday
96 Trolls - Poppy's Party
97 The Ugly Duckling
98 Cars - Look Out for Mater!
99 101 Dalmatians
100 The Sorcerer's Apprentice
101 Tangled
102 Avengers – The Threat of Thanos
105 The Mighty Thor
106 Doctor Strange
107 Captain Marvel
108 The Invincible Iron Man
110 The Big Freeze
111 Ratatouille
112 Aladdin
113 Aladdin - I am the Genie
114 Seven Dwarfs Find a House
115 Toy Story
116 Toy Story 4
117 Paw Patrol - Jurassic Bark!
118 Paw Patrol - Mighty Pup Power!
121 The Lion King - I am Simba
122 Winnie the Pooh - The Honey Tree
123 Frozen II
124 Baby Shark and the Colours of the Ocean
125 Baby Shark and the Police Sharks!
126 Trolls World Tour
127 I am Elsa
128 I am Anna
129 I am Olaf
130 I am Mulan
131 Sleeping Beauty
132 Onward
133 Paw Patrol – Puppy Birthday to You!
134 Black Widow
135 Trolls – Poppy's Big Day!
136 Baby Shark and the Tooth Fairy
137 Baby Shark – Mummy Shark
138 Inside Out
139 The Prince and the Pauper
140 Finding Dory
142 The Lion King - Simba's Daring Rescue

•Book list may be subject to change. Not all titles are listed.

TCS